LANDMARKS IN HISTORY

THE NORMAN CONQUEST

IVAN LAPPER • CHRISTOPHER GRAVETT

OSPREY
PUBLISHING

Contents

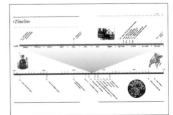

Introduction

IVAN LAPPER ARCA has established himself as a leading illustrator in the field of historical reconstruction. His work, particularly his architectural and landscape impressions, may be seen in museums, historic buildings and ancient monuments across Britain. Ivan Lapper uses archaeological and documentary evidence to make cardboard models, from which the final artwork is created.

CHRISTOPHER GRAVETT is Senior Curator at the Royal Armouries and a recognised authority on the arms, armour and warfare of the medieval world. He has worked as an advisor for numerous TV and Film productions.

The year 1066 is one of the most pivotal dates in English history. In that year, William the Bastard invaded from Normandy, seized the crown and became the first Norman king of England. Unlike the Viking invasions that had preceded it the Norman Conquest brought lasting changes in government, culture and language, shaping the way we think and our attitudes right up to the present day. England now entered Europe at centre stage.

The Conquest was recorded in an amazing piece of pictorial history, the Bayeux Tapestry, which has come down to us as a unique reminder of the events of 1066. Only by standing at one end of this amazing work can one really appreciate it. Gazing down its length is remarkable enough yet when one reaches the end of the room in which it is displayed, the Tapestry curves round and continues up the other side. Historians still argue over its content, its meaning, where it was made and who made it. In this book I hope to highlight some of the many problems in its interpretation. It is a rare document and must be used with caution.

The Norman Conquest was the last successful invasion of England by a foreign claimant. Others have tried – such as the Spanish, the French, the Germans – and failed. We can therefore look back on the Norman Conquest as helping to shape the England of the present. The importance of 1066 is seen in the permanence of those changes.

With special thanks to the City of Bayeux for permission to reproduce all details and scenes from the Bayeux Tapestry included in this book. (The Bayeux Tapestry, 11th century)

Anglo-Saxon England

Edward the Confessor holding a sceptre, from the Bayeux Tapestry

*E*ngland in the 11th century was a rich prize. The land held about one and a half million people, Anglo-Saxons with large settlements of Vikings – mainly Danes – across north and eastern England. In the Celtic west were the Cornish and Welsh, with Scots and Picts on the northern borders.

The kingship was strong, with the king as war-leader, anointed by the church and assisted by his council or *witan*. He could raise the geld, a form of land tax, and had rights to bridge building, service on town fortifications (*burhs*), and military service in the *fyrd* (the king's army). His most powerful subjects were the earls, then the king's thegns and lesser thegns.

Much of England was a rural economy. *Sokemen* were freemen who paid rents for their land but many villagers could not leave without the lord's permission. Slaves also existed, largely in the west and south.

Towns were expanding and London was a major centre, still protected by its Roman walls. Moreover, the coinage was strong, with mints under royal control. The church had experienced a monastic revival in the 10th century, which was now ebbing. English art – painting, ivory carving, sculpture and needlework – was of a very high order.

Edward the Confessor, had to contend with a few very powerful earls. In the midlands was Edwin of Mercia and to the north his brother, Morcar of Northumbria. In the south the most powerful was Harold Godwinsson of Wessex, with his younger brothers, Gyrth in East Anglia and Leofwine to the north of London. The king was married to Harold's sister, but there were no children and thus no heir.

The Normans

A Norman woodcutter, who appears to be left-handed

T he Duchy of Normandy was nominally held from the French king. Founded by the Viking, Rollo, in 911, the Normans (i.e. northmen) soon adopted French ways, customs and language, even their methods of fighting from horseback.

The old capital was Rouen but William the Bastard had moved his power-base westwards to Caen. Thanks to an inherited Carolingian tradition, the introduction of feudalism, a thriving economy and large ducal estates, William was a strong ruler, related to many of his leading nobles. The local officials, or *vicomtes*, assisted in imposing the Duke's justice, a growing force at this time, and farmed fixed revenues for their estates. William was able to impose direct tax, as well as tolls, feudal dues and profits from justice. He called councils of varying sizes, the largest of which included all his magnates, ecclesiastical and lay. Charters were produced in numbers that compare well with England.

Unlike England, Normandy was a feudal state, that is, one based on land held in return for military service, for which vassals did homage to their lord, both lay and ecclesiastical. Thus the land, lordship and knight service were inextricably bound together. Some families held *allodial* land, free from ducal control; some held land from several lords, or might enfeof more knights than were necessary for ducal service; William could not impose as complete a rule as he might have wished.

Together with the mounted and fully armed knight went the use of castles by the Duke and his magnates. These residential strongholds, unlike the communal *burhs* of England, were often of earth and timber construction, but already a few large stone towers, or *donjons*, had been erected, such as the now vanished ducal example in Rouen. Once in power William strove to ensure that no castles should be erected without his agreement, and that all those held by magnates should be open to him as required.

The Norman church was experiencing the same impetus which had affected the English church the previous century. It welcomed foreigners able to prove their worth and several great monastic houses flourished, notably the abbey of Bec, and produced distinguished churchmen. William would later use the contrast with England as propaganda in citing his cause to Rome. In 1047 William introduced the Truce of God to enforce his peace. However, he made sure that his bishops owed him military service for the lands they held.

Norman towns were encouraged and founded by magnates. Indeed, the duchy was well ahead in the economic expansion of Europe, maintaining trade connections with Scandinavia and with London. The dukes were careful to control the coinage, and the vigorous economy made Normandy a rich part of northern France.

Trees are felled and planks shaped as new ships are built for invasion. (The Bayeux Tapestry, 11th century. With special permission of the City of Bayeux)

William
the Bastard

William in state, a sheathed sword resting on his shoulder

William was born at Falaise in about 1027 or 1028, the illegitimate son of Duke Robert the Magnificent and Herleve, usually thought to be a tanner's daughter. When Robert died on pilgrimage in 1035, the young William several times narrowly escaped death at the hands of enemies who had no wish to accept him as rightful duke. However, with the help of a number of close allies he managed to survive and, assisted by the French king, Henry I, defeated a coalition of rebels at the battle of Val-ès-Dunes in 1047. As he strengthened his grip on Normandy he faced aggression from Henry, now worried by his vassal's increasing power. Aided by the Count of Anjou, Henry pushed into Normandy only to be defeated at Mortemer in 1054. A similar invasion in 1057 ended when the French rearguard was cut off and destroyed at the ford at Varaville. When both Henry and the count of Anjou died in 1060, William was given a respite from pressure on these borders. However, he had never commanded in a pitched battle before Hastings, and had fought only in two.

William was an impressive figure. A single surviving thighbone from his tomb at Caen suggests a man about 5 feet 8 inches tall, above average for his day. He married Matilda, daughter of the count of Flanders, probably in 1051, despite initial objections to the match, thus securing an ally on his eastern flank. Matilda was a diminutive figure but an able consort, producing two future kings of England, William Rufus and Henry I.

William seems to have had enough charisma to convince his magnates to support his invasion plans. By sending Lanfranc of

Bec to plead his case in Rome he managed to have the invasion of England labelled as a crusade, and to obtain a papal banner from Pope Alexander II. His nature had a ruthless streak and he well knew when to use it to speed an enemy to surrender. At the siege of Alençon in 1051 he cut off the hands and feet of those who insulted his birth.

The relationship between the English and Norman ruling houses came from Emma, sister of William's grandfather, who married King Ethelred of England. Their sons, Alfred and Edward, were sent to the Norman court for safety as the Danes overran England. Here Edward grew up with Norman ways until he succeeded to the English throne in 1042. Norman chroniclers assert that the childless Edward had promised William the crown, and it is just possible that the Duke visited England in 1051. According to the Bayeux Tapestry, Earl Harold visited Normandy, probably in 1064 or 1065, presumably to confirm William's succession. Whether Edward changed his mind on his deathbed will never be known, but he may have decided England would not accept a Norman on the throne. Unfortunately, the Normans did not recognise such changes of mind once an oath was made, and William still considered himself rightful king.

Silver penny of William I as King of England. Royal control was important; this example was minted in Hereford. (Courtesy of the Trustees of the British Museum)

King Harold

King Harold holding the sword and sceptre

Harold II was born in about 1021, the second son of Godwin, Earl of Wessex, who had been raised by King Cnut (1016-1035). His mother was Gytha, Cnut's sister, which explains why the first four sons of Godwin bore Danish names.

When Godwin died in 1053 his eldest son was already dead and Harold inherited Wessex. Harold's brother, Tostig, ruled Northumbria before being turned out by the people. Two other brothers, Gyrth and Leofwine, ruled earldoms, while their younger brother, Wulfnoth, had been a hostage in the Norman court since Godwin's revolt in 1051. Harold's sister, Edith, was Edward's queen; presumably Godwin hoped that through her his family would put a king on the English throne.

There is not a great deal of evidence for Harold's physical appearance. The 13th-century chronicler, Snorri, makes King Harald Hardrada of Norway observe the English king as a small man who stood well in his stirrups, but then Hardrada was apparently very tall.

Harold seems to have been a skilful commander. In 1055 he led an army to stop the privations of King Gruffydd of North Wales, building a *burh* round Hereford and organising the burghers for military service. In 1062 he led a force from Gloucester in mid winter, crossing the Dee and seizing Gruffydd's headquarters at Rhuddlan. He followed up the next year by leading a fleet from Bristol while Tostig brought forces round from the north. Noting the way the Welsh dressed, Harold ordered his men to use javelins and lighter armour rather than mail coats, in order to negotiate the rugged terrain better. This pressure caused Gruffydd to be killed by his own men and his head to be brought to the Earl. Harold had shown his flair for swift action, which he used again in 1066. Faced with the invasion by Harald Hardrada and Tostig in September of that year, he abandoned his south coast watch and marched 190 miles in five days, before beating the Vikings at Stamford Bridge in Yorkshire. He then marched his men back to London, resting only a few days before marching into Sussex and his confrontation with the Normans, who had meanwhile landed. Though he may have intended to charge into William's camp at Hastings, his choice of a ridge with steep flanks as a defensive position nearly proved too much for William's army.

Godwin obviously had pretensions for his family but Harold, not being of English royal blood, may not have planned to take the crown even during his visit to Normandy. The chroniclers dispute whether Edward finally chose him. However, nomination by the monarch was not the sole criterion for becoming king. The assent of the *witan* was also required, and Harold was the best man to staunch any attempts at invasion by other claimants.

Harold is offered the crown then appears at his coronation, with Archbishop Stigand at his side. (The Bayeux Tapestry, 11th century. With special permission of the City of Bayeux)

The Norman Conquest

A ship joining the fleet

Edward the Confessor died on 5 January 1066. He was buried the following day, when Harold was crowned king. William sent Lanfranc to Rome to obtain papal backing. He called his magnates to councils, but it was necessary in many cases to use force of personality, together with offers of land to be won in England.

On 24 April, Halley's Comet blazed for a week in the sky. An omen to many, it appears on the Tapestry near a worried Harold. The estuary of the River Dives became the assembly place for the fleet, said to number 696 vessels, while the troops began to assemble nearby, but the wind blew obstinately from a northerly direction. Harold was guarding family lands in the south, while an English fleet, said to consist of 700 ships, patrolled the Channel.

On 8 September the English army ran out of provisions and the fleet was ordered to London to refit. William took this opportunity to move his ships some 160 miles eastwards along the coast to Saint Valéry-sur-Somme, but several vessels were lost in storms. Meanwhile, Harold had waited. In early September came the threat from Harald Hardrada of Norway. Landing with Tostig in the Humber, he defeated Edwin and Morcar's army at Gate Fulford outside York on 20 September and demanded hostages. Harold raced north, surprised the Norsemen on 25 September and cut them to pieces at Stamford Bridge. Hardrada and Tostig were killed, but the south lay unprotected.

The chroniclers assert that the wind did not change direction until about 27 September. However, William may have deliberately waited until the English army went north, before embarking. The horses were presumably loaded using ramps, the ships being brought up at high tide, which was at about 15:20 GMT.

The
Landing

At Pevensey, Norman war-horses are jumped from a ship

The fleet left before sunset, probably about 17:00GMT, well before low tide, assisted by outflowing currents. Apparently William's ship, the *Mora*, a gift from his wife, moved so fast that it lost sight of the others, so he dropped anchor and called for a feast aboard, to allay fears. As they waited, the ships came up. Two ships were blown off course, to land near Old Romney, where their crews were killed by the English. The rest of the ships crossed safely and, early next morning the fleet arrived off Pevensey. In 1066 the town with its Roman fortress lay on a spit of land on the west side of a large tidal lagoon with mud flats. The mouth of the lagoon was partly closed by a shingle bank. It is not clear where the fleet disembarked. There was a harbour, probably with wharves, by the north wall of the fort, and William's ship, the horse transports and garrison vessels may have made for this. Some may have come into the lagoon and beached on the flats at low tide, or else along the shingle. When William landed he stumbled and fell, a bad omen, but a knight nearby told him he had the earth of England in his hands.

There was no opposition, for Harold was still in the north. The Normans erected a perhaps prefabricated timber castle in the Roman fortress. It may have been the same day or that following when William moved the army eastwards to Hastings. The town lay on a peninsula between two marshy river estuaries, ideal for a protected camp similar to the Viking habit of camping on an island and the only dry route was a prehistoric track running north between the two river valleys.

William now set about devastating the area, not only to bring in food, but to lure Harold south to avenge his people.

Marching to Battle

Mailed English thegns or Anglo-Danish housecarls defend their position

Harold marched south but only waited five or six days in London for fresh troops, probably leaving again on 11 October. He marched via Rochester before coming to the area north of the Hastings peninsula, some eight miles from the town. Here, by the crossroads at Caldbec Hill, where stood an apple tree, the English army halted on the evening of 13 October.

Norman scouts having brought news of the approaching enemy, William ordered his men to stand to arms. At daybreak, at about 5:20 GMT, the army began marching out towards the English. By the time they reached the slopes of Telham Hill they could see the English ahead, forming up on the opposite ridge. The Norman move apparently caught Harold by surprise and he was still ordering his troops when the Normans marched down into the valley, actually a saddle between two brooks.

In front rose the ridge of Senlac Hill, like a hammer-head whose shaft forms a neck of land running back towards Caldbec Hill, a mile to the north. Along the crest stood the English line, perhaps as many as 8,000 men in ten ranks. Harold stood near the point where the track crossed the ridge, the gold embroidered banner of the Fighting Man beside him, and the windsock dragon banner of Wessex seen on the Tapestry. Around him and forming part of the front line were housecarls and king's thegns, the best troops, wearing mail, many with two-handed axes. Lesser thegns formed the bulk of the troops, with levies in rear.

Today the ridge is partly covered by the buildings of the abbey William founded, and the slope somewhat altered by the necessity of placing buildings. Nevertheless, on the west side of the valley can be seen the hillock which appears to figure on the Tapestry, and below it the pools created when the monks dammed the stream for fishponds. The eastern end of the ridge is difficult to determine; the English line could have extended between 600 and 800 yards.

William may have had some 7,500 men. The first division wheeled left and formed up on the western side of the field, mainly composed of Bretons. The largest contingent was that of the Normans in the centre. The right wing included many French mercenaries. Archers, some crossbowmen and perhaps a few slingers made up the front line, though only archers are shown on the Tapestry. They were mainly unarmoured, but behind came large numbers of mailed infantry. In rear trotted William's best troops, his squadrons of mounted mailed knights.

At about 9:00GMT the battle began with the terrible sound of trumpets.

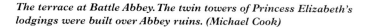

The terrace at Battle Abbey. The twin towers of Princess Elizabeth's lodgings were built over Abbey ruins. (Michael Cook)

The Battle of Hastings

An unarmoured Norman archer takes aim

The Bretons on the left have fled and confusion is spreading in the Norman army. Duke William pushes his helmet back to show that he is still alive. His half-brother, Odo, is shown helping to stem the panic. (Angus McBride)

he Norman archers walked forward and loosed a cloud of arrows, but many hit the English wall of shields or passed over the heads of the whole army. Both sides relied on shooting the enemy's arrows back at them, but the English had few archers to shoot back so the Normans soon ran short of ammunition. This Norman 'softening up' barrage failed to have much impact, so the infantry was sent forward. Coming up the slope they were met by a blizzard of missiles: javelins, small axes, arrows, even stones tied to pieces of wood. On closing there followed a ferocious hand-to-hand struggle, in which the Normans suffered particularly from the English axes. Squadrons of Norman cavalry now came up in support, not in a concerted charge but in groups, throwing spears or thrusting with them, only a few tucking them under the arm.

After a time, the Bretons on the left wing broke and fled back down the slope. Unarmoured Englishmen chased after them. Some Norman horsemen got into difficulties by riding over the hillock in the valley and into the marshy area beyond. This was the crisis of the battle. William himself was unhorsed, the left wing in flight, the centre and right now giving ground. Remounting, he pushed the helmet back from his face to show his presence. With Eustace of Boulogne carrying the papal banner William rode among his soldiers shouting that he was alive. Then he led some cavalry from the centre, cutting down the Englishmen caught in the open. The crisis had passed, and both sides regrouped.

Many more mounted Norman knights were used in the following assaults, but they met with no more success than previously. According to the contemporary William of Poitiers, William twice ordered feigned flights by groups of cavalry to draw Englishmen out, inspired by the earlier rout of the Bretons; the horsemen outstripped their pursuers then wheeled about. However, as the afternoon wore on the English still held the ridge. The numbers of dead now made an additional barrier, and many knights had lost their horses and were fighting on foot. In the lower border of the Tapestry increasing numbers of archers now appear, their quivers in front of them. It seems that fresh supplies of arrows had now arrived, and the archers shot before the mixed infantry and cavalry again attacked. At some point in this final phase, an arrow struck Harold in or near the right eye. The English line was by now much weakened and had drawn in its flanks so that at last a body of Norman knights managed to reach the end of the line, and began to roll it up. Others broke through the English line and attacked the standards. Harold was cut down and killed, the Dragon banner felled and the Fighting Man carried off, later to be sent to Rome.

William pushes his helmet back to show he is alive, as Eustace of Boulogne (pointing) carries the sacred banner. (The Bayeux Tapestry, 11th century. With special permission of the City of Bayeux)

Holding the Prize

The windsock dragon banner of Harold, cut down at Hastings

The Battle of Hastings was a close-run thing. The struggle had lasted much of the autumn day, much longer than most medieval battles. William retired to his base at Hastings and after five days he set out for London, marching first eastwards to Dover, which surrendered and was fortified with a castle, then to Canterbury, which also surrendered. He struck westwards, skirting London but sending a detachment to probe the defences. Vigorously rebuffed at Southwark, the army continued west, obtaining the submission of Winchester; William had thus already captured the main port, ecclesiastical capital and capital of Wessex. Crossing the Thames at Wallingford (also given a castle) he marched in a great threatening sweep well to the north of London, finally receiving its surrender at Little Berkhamsted in Hertfordshire. He set about building castles in the city, the Tower being the most famous, and was crowned king of England on Christmas Day, 1066.

Revolts soon manifested themselves. After William returned to Normandy in spring, 1067, Edric the Wild attacked in Herefordshire, but was beaten off. William's one-time ally, Eustace of Boulogne, landed near Dover but was also routed. William returned, only to face revolt in Exeter in spring, 1068. This he quelled and built a castle there. Matilda now came over to be crowned as queen. However, Earls Edwin and Morcar, together with the young royal claimant Edgar, began to threaten in the north. William advanced, planting castles at Warwick, Nottingham and York itself. On his return march he also placed castles in Lincoln, Huntington and Cambridge.

In January 1069 a rising in Durham and York caused him again to march rapidly north, this time planting a second castle on the other bank of the River Ouse. Edgar was forced to retire to Scotland, and William returned south, only to find a Danish fleet appear off the east coast and pillage its way up to the Humber. Trouble was once more fomented in Yorkshire, Edgar reappeared, and in the west revolts broke out in Devon, Cornwall, Dorset, Somerset and Cheshire. Leaving his subordinates to deal with the west, William once more marched north. The Danes were eventually bought off, and the king entered York. There followed the devastation of parts of the north in retribution. The crisis had passed; he outmanoeuvred Hereward the Wake in the Fens in 1070-71 and in 1072 took a land and sea force to Scotland to persuade King Malcolm to become his vassal. England was effectively subdued.

One of the two mottes erected by William in York in 1068-69, with Clifford's Tower, added in the 13th century.

The Use of Castles

The stone donjon at the ducal palace in Rouen

The 11th-century stone hall at Chepstow Castle, Gwent, later heightened, was built by William FitzOsbern, close friend of William the Conqueror.

One of the major weapons in William's armoury was his abundant use of castles. A castle was a fortification and a home for a lord, be he noble or king. England was dotted with *burhs*, large fortifications which might surround a town, often of earth and timber, but these were communal defences, not private dwellings. Edward the Confessor had introduced castles with his Norman favourites, but these were few in number.

Whenever William came to a place of sufficient importance, he planted a castle. Often this was in a town, and might necessitate pulling down a number of houses once the Norman engineers had selected the best site. Most of the castles of the day were of earth and timber. This meant that they could be erected in a matter of weeks or months, a useful attribute in a hostile land. English labour was employed, probably utilising the king's right to *burh* work. The simplest form was the defended enclosure, now called a 'ringwork'. The area to be defended was surrounded by a ditch, the earth from which was placed on the inner edge to form a bank. This was then topped with a stout palisade of upright wooden posts. Inside were all the buildings necessary for a self-sufficient unit, including a hall, kitchen, stables, storehouses, workshops, and a well. Some castles additionally had a mound of earth at one side, the 'motte', which carried a palisade on the flattened summit and a building within it. The latter could be used as a hall on larger examples, or else as a watchtower and last-ditch defence. Such 'motte and bailey' castles are shown on the Bayeux Tapestry at Dinan, Dol, Rennes and Bayeux, though not all sites have evidence for such. At Hastings the motte, with rammed earth layers, is shown under construction. Again, the surviving motte does not show this type of construction, though the original remains of the motte may be inside.

The Tapestry shows William in council at his palace at Rouen. Here was a large stone tower or *donjon* (now destroyed) which may have been the inspiration for the surviving *donjon* at the Tower of London. At this time such 'keeps' were never numerous in Normandy or England, as they were expensive and slow to build. However, being of stone they were resistant to fire, though many may have been used as symbols of power, and for ceremonial or social functions, far more than defence. Stone was gradually used more and more, to replace the palisades on the motte (producing the so-called 'shell keep') and the bailey defences. The castle had come to stay.

The building of the White Tower, the donjon in the Tower of London, about 1080. The castle was placed in the south east corner of the old Roman city wall, the other sides protected by ditch and palisades.

Government

A mailed Norman knight, the elite of the feudal army

William preserved much English government machinery, partly because of practical necessity, because the Normans were always ready to adapt what they found, and because he considered himself the legitimate successor to the English crown. There was, however, the almost complete imposition of a new, French-speaking group of officials, who looked not to Scandinavia but across the Channel to France. The lands of defeated Englishmen were parcelled out, which explains why lords, even the king, had scattered estates. By the end of William's reign in 1087 there were only two Englishmen of any consequence left in nobility, and only three prelates.

The Normans took over the use of the sealed writ, soon being written in Latin to conform with continental methods. The royal seal had shown the king on both sides seated in majesty; now one side was replaced by the king as a mounted knight. The introduction of feudalism saw the English *witan* replaced by the council of William's tenants-in-chief. A specific treasury now appeared; the king accrued wealth from the geld, but also from additional crown lands, feudal dues and increasing profits of justice. In the early 12th century come the first references to the Exchequer. The king now had two lands to govern, and so the new post of chief justiciar makes its appearance in English government, its incumbent to rule in the king's stead when absent. Similarly the chancellor appears, head of an itinerant chancery. The Normans kept the basic system of local government also. William did not impose his *vicomtes* as in Normandy; instead, he utilised the English shire reeves, or sheriffs. With the great earls gone the sheriffs became powerful royal servants, the king's representative in the shires, usually being based in the castle of the county town. Legal cases were held in the shire court. At first William made no move to remove English officials and probably wished for a genuine Anglo-Norman kingdom, since he was patient with the surviving English nobles. However, honorial courts were a new feudal institution. At local level, the hundred courts continued. New laws, including the *murdrum* fine for killing Frenchmen and the judicial duel imported from Normandy, were added to a legal system invigorated by the Normans, such as in the centralisation of hearing pleas.

William inherited a rich country and made certain that he controlled the rights to mint money, the dies in London being changed to his name. Foreign magnates wishing to stamp their authority, and to increase their resources, set up new boroughs, often next to one of their castles.

William depicted as a mounted knight and leader of the feudal host, on the reverse of his great seal. The obverse shows him seated on his throne with orb and sceptre. (Public Records Office, London)

A New Way of Life

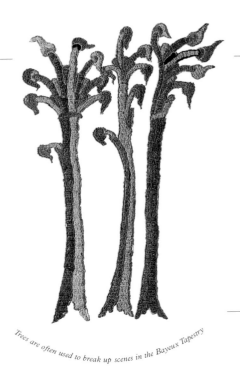

Trees are often used to break up scenes in the Bayeux Tapestry

A feudal society was imposed on England. In return for land the king could expect quotas of knights from his tenants-in-chief, together with monetary aid, 'reliefs' (inheritance money) and wardship of minors. In theory a feudal army of about 5,000 knights could be raised, and William also retained the English *fyrd*. Tenants-in-chief similarly granted land to their own vassals. No land was without a lord and all belonged to the king, William being able to impose a much firmer hold on England than Normandy. The feudal contract by homage and oath, knight service and castle-guard, were all part of the new way of life.

Although Englishmen of rank remained in their posts they were acutely aware that they were now the aliens in top society. The English were seen as underdogs. Norman French became the language of the court until the 15th century, but a modified English eventually won the day. English children were given Norman names such as Robert and Richard as parents aspired to join the new order. William created the New Forest (including woods and common) for his pleasure and imposed harsh forest laws across England; villages within such areas were subject to it.

At Christmas 1085 William ordered a survey of his kingdom, which so amazed people that it became known as the Domesday survey, because everything was known as on the day of judgement. London and Winchester are not covered, nor is much of the north, but three volumes hold minute details such as the numbers of ploughs in a village, all for purposes of taxation. The clerks introduced the word 'manor', at this time simply meaning the dwelling of an important person. It is a unique surviving record.

The Church Reforms

Stigand, the excommunicated Archbishop of Canterbury deposed by William

The Anglo-Saxon church was rich but not as needful of reform as Norman propaganda had suggested, though corruption was a problem. Stigand, the excommunicate archbishop of Canterbury, may well have crowned Harold, but there were worthy prelates in England. After the Conquest, increasing numbers of foreigners were placed in posts vacated by Englishmen. The wealth of the church was a magnet for potential recruits.

Though Stigand and two other bishops were deposed, William did not forcibly remove churchmen. However, he was a keen reformer, and replacements for vacant sees were inevitably found from across the Channel. Most notable was Lanfranc of Bec, who became Archbishop of Canterbury. A close friend of William, the two men had a partnership that would not be repeated for centuries. Lanfranc brought a group of followers and pupils, all worthy of office. Ecclesiastical councils were revived, separate ecclesiastical jurisdiction allowed, and the church began to regard itself as a separate body from the state. While Lanfranc and the group of Norman prelates felt bound to William (often by feudal ties for knight service) and co-operated with his reforming zeal, this course would eventually cause problems, with the church regarding itself as beyond state control.

The monasteries also received new blood. Lanfranc had been Prior of Bec and so it is not surprising that he was keen to see improvements in English monasticism. He compiled his *Consuetudines* for his monks at Christ Church but this spread to many other houses. Monks were drawn from the new ruling classes, and two major new houses were founded, at Battle, site of William's victory, and at Lewes in Sussex. There was also a great upsurge in monasticism in the north. From France came books and learning which had been somewhat lacking in England, and a familiarity with the Latin language that allowed far better intercourse with the continent.

Numerous ecclesiastical buildings survive with Romanesque work preserved in their fabric. English architecture had not been particularly remarkable for its size, and had often been constructed in timber. The Normans used stone far more than their predecessors. These buildings, like the castles, left an indelible stamp on the landscape. Except for Westminster and Waltham in Essex, nearly every major church was rebuilt by the Normans, now larger and on a more impressive scale than formerly. The nobility poured money into pious foundations and building programmes, on a scale not known before the Conquest. Even the Anglo-Saxon Wulfstan of Worcester felt it necessary to pull down his old church and rebuild in the new style, though he wept to see it done.

The imposing early 12th century nave of Durham Cathedral, with typically massive pillars. (Dean and Chapter of Durham Cathedral)

What is the Bayeux Tapestry?

Halley's Comet, as depicted in the Bayeux Tapestry

The Bayeux Tapestry is a unique survival from the 11th century, 70.34 m (230 ft 10 ¼in) by 50 cm (19 ¾in). It should be noted at the outset that it is not strictly speaking a tapestry, woven on a loom. Rather, it consists of a bleached linen background on to which scenes are embroidered using needle and thread. Indeed, when first mentioned in 1476 it is referred to as an embroidery, but in 1730 the French antiquary, Montfaucon, already speaks of a tapestry. This was reinforced when it was exhibited in Paris in 1803-04.

The Tapestry covers the entire story of the Conquest, beginning with an aging King Edward sending Harold to Normandy, who is seized by Count Guy of Ponthieu and rescued by Duke William. He is taken on a campaign to quieten unrest in Brittany and rescues two Norman soldiers from the river Couesnon. He is rewarded with Norman armour in a scene heavy with the symbolism of a lord making a new vassal. Back at Bayeux he takes a sacred oath to help William before returning to England. The death and funeral of Edward, shown transposed to emphasize the swiftness of Harold's seizure of the throne, are followed by a picture of the new king in state. The appearance of Halley's comet in the next scene is brilliantly used to contrast a bowed Harold, with ghostly invasion ships below. The Norman response is then depicted: the building of a fleet, the carrying of provisions to the ships, the crossing to England, and finally the great battle at Hastings. The borders of the Tapestry carry little scenes often symbolically relevant to the main picture, but in the battle the dead and dying break into the lower border. The Tapestry ends with the flight of the English but damage has caused the loss of perhaps two further panels. If the tapestry described in the work of the 12th-century writer, Baudri of Bourgueil is believed, they showed the capture of cities (perhaps London) and lastly the coronation of William, thus balancing nicely the opening sequence with Edward the Confessor on his throne.

The Bayeux Tapestry tells the story of the Norman Conquest from the point of view of the conquerors themselves, lacking the fiction that soon began to creep into the various accounts of 1066. Moreover, English and Norman chroniclers do not always agree on, or are silent about, parts of the story of the Conquest. That is not to say the Tapestry is a true version of events. It must never be forgotten that it was made to show what its patron wanted it to show.

In the 19th century the Tapestry was renovated. Already in 1730 it appears that large margins of linen were added as backing because the edges were deteriorating. In 1842 Edouard Lambert, librarian at Bayeux, had it restored for exhibition in the library. A comparison of Montfaucon's drawings of 1730 with Charles Stothard's plates of 1819 and the 1873 hand-coloured photographs also serves to highlight the repairs. These were mainly done over the scenes of Count Guy and the end scenes of fleeing Englishmen.

The Bayeux Tapestry displayed in a purpose built museum at Bayeux in Normandy. The embroidery continues round a corner and back up the opposite side. (The Bayeux Tapestry, 11th century. With special permission of the City of Bayeux)

Who Created it and Why?

Bishop Odo brandishing a baculum, a wooden staff of authority

Who was the patron? Almost certainly Odo, Bishop of Bayeux, who also became Earl of Kent after the Conquest. Half-brother to William, he most probably had the impressive embroidery made to hang in his church at Bayeux, newly consecrated in 1077. Odo is prominently depicted, whether blessing a meal, sitting at the Duke's right hand during a council of war, or in armour rallying the panicking troops at Hastings. Several of his vassals – Wadard, Vital and Turold – may be those who appear by name in the Tapestry, lending support to the choice of this bishop as likely patron. It also helps to fix a probable date for the work. Odo was eventually imprisoned by William, probably for attempting to march on Rome, which would mean that the Tapestry was made before 1082, a period which also fits with the style of design. The form of embroidery, in laid and couched work using wool, seems to be found mainly in northern Europe and declined at the end of the Romanesque period, while the long, narrative strip was an unusual form of hanging at later periods.

The style of illustration seen in the scenes on the Tapestry has been linked to English manuscripts. Several of the figures show similarities in their design or pose with those in Anglo-Saxon manuscripts, largely products of the Canterbury school of illumination, and, given that Odo was Earl of Kent, it is likely that the Tapestry was designed at Canterbury, possibly by an Englishman under Norman guidance. It is also likely that it was produced by English needle workers, whose work was prized in Europe for its quality. However, some authorities argue that the comparison with contemporary manuscripts points rather to a continental influence than an Anglo-Saxon one, especially since some features of Anglo-Saxon work were copied in continental manuscripts. This school favours a Norman origin, probably centred around Bayeux.

The Tapestry recounts a great historical narrative told from a Norman viewpoint, but it is also a moral tale, graphically illustrating how greed and the breaking of sacred oaths led Harold to his downfall and violent death. William is portrayed as the great crusader, who with God's help becomes the victor in a trial by battle. For that reason it was worthy to hang in a church. This form of hanging was not uncommon, and a number of such pieces are known from literary sources; they simply have not survived, or survive as fragments. The tradition that William's wife, Matilda, was responsible for the Tapestry is unlikely but understandable, given the actions of other rulers.

Odo rallies the young men during the crisis at Hastings. He may be wearing a padded coat, though it could be a type of garment only worn by men of rank. (The Bayeux Tapestry, 11th century. With special permission of the City of Bayeux)

How was it Made?

A winged lion; such beasts may have some symbolic meaning

The Tapestry was conceived by a designer who would have worked with the patron together with one or more others who related the story as it was to be told. The design would have to be laid out in cartoon form, to scale, with the borders and inscription fitted in. It was a monumental task. It has been calculated that there are 626 human figures, 190 horses or mules, 35 hounds or dogs, 506 other various animals, 37 ships, 33 buildings and 37 trees or groups of trees. This suggests that more than one artist was involved. The wool would have to be dyed in large amounts so as to match throughout, and spun ready for use. Frames were needed, since each scene would require the workers to have their hands free for the laid and couched work used in the Tapestry. Copper alloy needles were probably employed.

Eight strips of linen appear to have been used, each perhaps being given to a different workshop. The strips would presumably be stitched together when completed. There are five main colours, terracotta red, blue-green, sage-green, buff and blue. Less frequently used are dark green, yellow, and dark blue (almost black). In laid and couched work the threads are laid in a tight mass over a given area, such as a figure. A second layer of threads (usually the same colour) is laid at right angles over this, the threads slightly spaced apart, perhaps 1/8 in. These are couched down with the same thread that holds them. The outline of the contours is worked in stem or outline stitch, which is also used for thin lines such as lettering, border lines, some scroll-work, spears, hands, faces, and many fillings such as the mail armour (conventionally shown as huge roundels rather than tiny interlinked rings). The fact that hair and horses, etc. are not always in naturalistic colours simply reflects the few colours used.

The History

of the

Tapestry

The motte and tower at Bayeux

The Bayeux Tapestry probably hung round the nave of Odo's cathedral at Bayeux, being two narrow to be functional as a wall hanging in a hall, to keep warmth in. It is an amazing survivor. Bayeux cathedral was burned in 1105 during a campaign by the Conqueror's son, Henry I, and another fire in 1159 destroyed the old building. The inventory of the Cathedral Chapter of 1476 is the first to mention the embroidery, together with the coronation robes of William and Matilda, all having survived the Hundred Years War, when the cathedral changed hands several times. It was there noted that the Tapestry was hung round the nave every year from 1-14 July, which included the anniversary of the consecration of the cathedral, and the Feast of the Relics. The cathedral treasury was looted during the Religious Wars of the 16th century but again the Tapestry escaped.

In 1730 Montfaucon published it in his *Monuments de la Monarchie Française*, and in 1767 it was noted as hanging round the piers of the nave. However, in 1792 French revolutionaries took it from the sacristy and used it to cover a wagon, only being rescued by the sterling efforts of Lambert Lèonard-Leforestier, a council member. It nearly suffered a similar fate soon after, being earmarked for use on the Chariot of the Goddess of Reason. In 1803 Napoleon, contemplating an invasion of England, ordered it to Paris but soon returned it. From 1812 it was shown in the Hôtel de Ville in Bayeux, where it was held on a winch and unrolled as necessary. It came to the library in the town in 1842, but was briefly put in a zinc container when threatened by

Prussian forces during the Franco-Prussian War (1870-71). In 1913 it moved to a better building but at the outbreak of World War II in 1939 was placed in an air-raid shelter. The German invaders proposed to bring it again to Paris when another invasion of England was planned, but this was not done. However, during the Allied landings of 1944 the Tapestry was hastily removed to the Louvre, being returned in 1945. In 1948 it was placed in a permanent museum and is now displayed in a special gallery in the former Bishops' Palace.

The nave of Bayeux Cathedral, rebuilt in the mid-12th century

Prelude to Invasion

Earl Harold reaches out to touch the sacred reliquaries at his oath taking

William watches Harold swearing his oath on two reliquaries, that on the left portable, that on the right with what appears to be a bull's eye on top. (The Bayeux Tapestry, 11th century. With special permission of the City of Bayeux)

Because of the interpretation of numerous historians, a number of scenes in the Tapestry have been the centre of debate. One of the earliest shows the journey of Earl Harold to Normandy, which has been questioned because it finds mention in a number of Norman sources but not in a single English account. William of Poitiers, the contemporary panegyrist of William, says it was to confirm the succession to William. It is possible that the scene apparently showing Edward ordering Harold to go could be interpreted (to English viewers) as warning him against it. We see Harold given arms by William, a clear symbol in Norman eyes of his becoming William's vassal, his 'man'. The oath is taken at Bayeux on sacred relics, though two chroniclers, William of Poitiers and the 12th-century Orderic Vitalis, locate it at Bonneville-sur-Touques and Rouen respectively. Here we may see Odo twisting facts to enhance his own church. Poitiers also states that the oath was taken before the campaign, suggesting it was placed last on the Tapestry to heighten tension. David Bernstein has seen the bull's eye on one relic as symbolic of the death of Harold. Wace, writing *c*.1150-75, suggests Harold was tricked by the relics being covered. No such deceit is shown, but then would hardly be suggested. In any case, Harold was in effect a prisoner and had little choice in the matter. On his return, Edward appears to admonish Harold, who looks distinctly hangdog, a strange stance if he had carried out Edward's wishes. Perhaps we are to interpret this as Edward's displeasure at Harold for making firm deals with William, such as marrying his daughter, as alleged by certain chroniclers.

The clerk and Aelfgyva, one of the few women in the Tapestry. (The Bayeux Tapestry, 11th century. With special permission of the City of Bayeux)

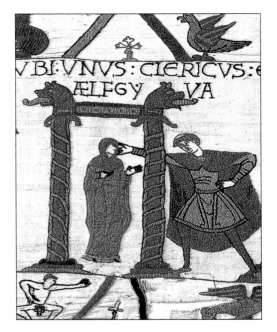

The scene showing the bequest by Edward on his deathbed has Harold and Stigand present, with Queen Edith at the old king's feet. What passed is now the subject of great argument and the Tapestry is silent on the matter. The left-facing funeral procession may echo the loss of smooth continuation by this coronation.

One of the most intriguing scenes in the Tapestry is that showing a woman and a clerk, the latter's hand touching her cheek. Above runs the legend: 'Where a certain clerk and Aelfgyva'. Today the meaning of this scene is lost but must have been fairly common knowledge at the time. It appears sandwiched between Harold's arrival at Rouen after being released from Count Guy, and the campaign against Brittany. A naked man in the lower border with obvious male attributes suggests some amoral story. Harold had a young sister called Aelfgifu, apparently betrothed to a Norman baron during his negotiations; was the Tapestry's insertion a social comment on her chastity?

Edward's funeral procession (left) precedes his burial. Above, his hand touches Harold's, perhaps a sign of his bequest. (The Bayeux Tapestry, 11th century. With special permission of the City of Bayeux)

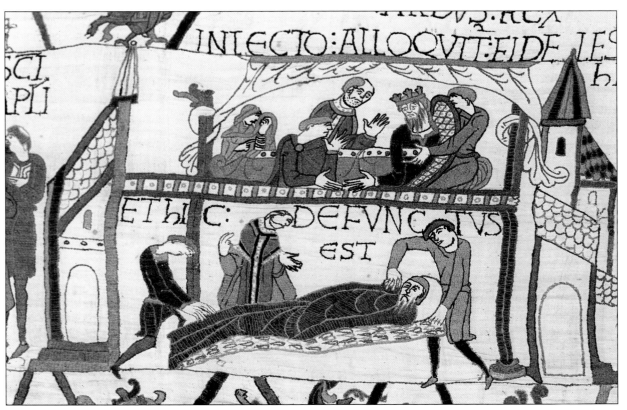

The Battle Scene

A mailed English warrior with a circular shield

The Norman horses step out of a vessel at Pevensey as the mast is unshipped. (The Bayeux Tapestry, 11th century. With special permission of the City of Bayeux)

The Tapestry has been scrutinised for clues about costume, armour and for the battle of Hastings. One dispute centres on the landing of the Norman horses. They are shown literally stepping out of the transports, which resemble the clinker-built Viking ships of the time. In 1963 Danish Sea Scouts, using a replica of the 9th-century Ladby ship, took horses on board and managed to jump them over the low gunwales of the ship in just this fashion. However, the replica was only taken along the coast and not tried in the open sea, where any noticeable swell would probably result in the horses being damaged or thrown overboard. Were deeper-bodied transports used in reality?

Depictions of armour also cause problems. The large, net-like appearance of the coats worn by both sides is today accepted as artistic licence for mail, which consisted of thousands of interlinked iron rings. The squares on the chests of some coats are usually now interpreted as flaps to cover the throat, or perhaps the neck opening. Three garments, however, seem to be covered in triangular shapes, variously interpreted as scale armour, padding, or a form of coat worn by high-ranking lords as a sort of badge (see pp. 32-33).

The battle scenes do not appear to include any heavy infantry among the Norman ranks, when Poitiers states they were present. This may reflect an aristocratic view that such people were only shown when of importance to the story, as were the archers.

The English line is shown with overlapping shields, illustrating the 'shield wall' of Anglo-Saxon poems. It may be that such a

The deaths of Harold's brothers, Gyrth and Leofwine, during the battle. (The Bayeux Tapestry, 11th century. With special permission of the City of Bayeux)

formation was broken up in order to use such weapons as the two-handed axe and the sword.

The scene showing English and French falling together in battle is usually accepted as the flight of the Bretons, with the hillock and reedy stream close by, though some think this represents the main ridge itself. The chaos is echoed by William portrayed pushing his helmet back to show he is alive, probably next to the papal banner. Odo is seen armed and rallying the fleeing horsemen in a prominent military role he may not have held in reality. The unarmoured Englishmen are probably those trapped by William's counterattack, and have led many to suggest this was an undisciplined rush by some fyrdmen. Gyrth and Leofwine appear dying in the panel before the debacle; were they leading a more serious counter-attack, and did their deaths deter their followers? It is also rather surprising that the brothers are shown together; it would be expected that they commanded their own troops at different parts of the line, unless this is simply artistic licence. No feigned flights are mentioned or obviously shown in the Tapestry.

Unarmoured English fyrdmen defend themselves at the hillock as Norman horsemen come to grief nearby. (The Bayeux Tapestry, 11th century. With special permission of the City of Bayeux)

The
Death of
Harold

The fall of King Harold at Hastings

The death of Harold has perhaps caused one of the greatest controversies over the Tapestry. A scene shows two figures, one holding an arrow shaft which has either struck in or near his eye and, to his right, a second figure falling under the sword of a Norman horseman. An inscription running above both figures reads: 'Here King Harold has been killed'.

It was assumed that, since the name 'Harold' appeared over the left-hand figure, this was the king being mortally wounded before being cut down. Then in 1960 C. Gibbs-Smith maintained that conventions of style meant the same person was never shown twice in the same scene, and that violent death is always represented by a falling figure. Therefore only the warrior being cut down could be Harold, and the arrow-in-the-eye story was born from a misreading of the Tapestry by Baudri of Bourgeuil, who describes a similar hanging in a 12th-century poem (1099-1102). However, in 1978, Brooks and Walker pointed out that conventions in fact showed that both figures could be Harold (note the dragon banner is shown twice in the scene, fallen and erect) and that Baudri, if indeed he did see the Tapestry, probably knew far more about conventions of style than do historians today. William of Malmesbury (writing *c.*1125) says the arrow pierced Harold's brain and he was then gashed by a sword as he lay prostrate, for which insult the knight responsible was dismissed from the army by William. It is worth noticing that the rider attacking the second figure has a sword close to his thigh. Malmesbury almost certainly knew the Tapestry and, if he

The figure struck in or near his eye, with 'Harold' written above. (The Bayeux Tapestry, 11th century. With special permission of the City of Bayeux)

did not, then the story of Harold being struck by the arrow and then cut down was current in England by 1125. Wace (*c*.1150-75) gives much detail, saying that the arrow struck Harold below the right eye, and that in his agony he broke the shaft before being hacked down. Much of this scene was damaged, but study of Stothard's illustrations, made in 1819 before restoration, shows an arrow and moustache on the falling figure; close inspection of the linen itself also reveals a row of stitch holes by the eye of the falling figure, reinforcing this argument.

Exactly who killed the king is less certain. The Carmen de Hastingae Proelio, whose 11th-century date is by no means wholly accepted, names William himself as having broken in and killed the king. If this were true, it would have been well publicised, yet the Duke's own panegyrist, William of Poitiers, is silent on the matter, saying only that Harold was killed. So is the Tapestry, which surely would have trumpeted this news.

In the lower border, men strip the dead of their mail. The latter appear naked, but other figures demonstrate that clothes are obviously worn beneath, and their appearance is almost certainly the result of restoration.

Harold is cut down by a Norman knight. (The Bayeux Tapestry, 11th century. With special permission of the City of Bayeux)

Legacy

Building the motte at Hastings

The Norman Conquest changed the course of English history, dragging England into mainstream Europe. The links forged with Normandy and the marriages of William's children led to a great Angevin Empire in the 12th century, stretching from Scotland to the Pyrenees. It also led to the loss of Normandy in 1204 and subsequent struggles with France in the Hundred Years War of the 14th and 15th centuries. Customary rivalry did not stop until the alliances forged in the 19th century and after. Trade was largely in wool, exported to the Low Countries for weaving into cloth. This love-hate relationship with Europe has continued until today.

The government has changed immensely since the Conquest but sheriffs still preside in counties. The chancery and exchequer remain common words on public lips, though the accounting systems have been somewhat updated. The laws rigorously enforced by the Normans have been augmented and improved upon enormously but England is still thick with ancient rights and regulations. The royal mint, which became until the 19th century based in the royal fortress of the Tower of London, still functions. Some consider that William introduced the first form of income tax.

The New Forest is the best monument to the Norman desire to preserve the game for royal hunting. It may be argued that, had the kings not had such a vested interest in preserving the deer and other wildlife for their own sport, some species would have disappeared long ago. Many other forests have been heavily thinned, often for ship-building, but remain in name, as do parks and chases. French place names, Christian and surnames abound, and many French words have entered our language.

Perhaps the most obvious legacy are the numerous churches, abbeys, cathedrals and castles throughout our countryside and towns. Some religious buildings have been partly concealed or destroyed by subsequent rebuilding but still function as centres of worship. Many castles are ruinous, indeed some now survive only as grassy earthworks, mute testament to their former importance.

However, in all this the Norman Conquest did not produce a simple overlay of one society upon another. It may be argued that the Angevin kingship introduced with Henry II in 1154 brought more of a French influence, because by then it was more defined. Yet the French still regard the English as Anglo-Saxons. The Normans brought new ideas, took over and improved where necessary, and left alone anything working efficiently. Gradually they themselves were assimilated into the society they conquered. The legacy of the Conquest is a blend of old, new and augmented institutions, thoughts and beliefs, which has helped to produce the Britain of today.

The White Tower of London, the donjon begun by William probably around 1077 but not finished until about 1100. (By special permission of the Trustees of the Armouries)

Timeline

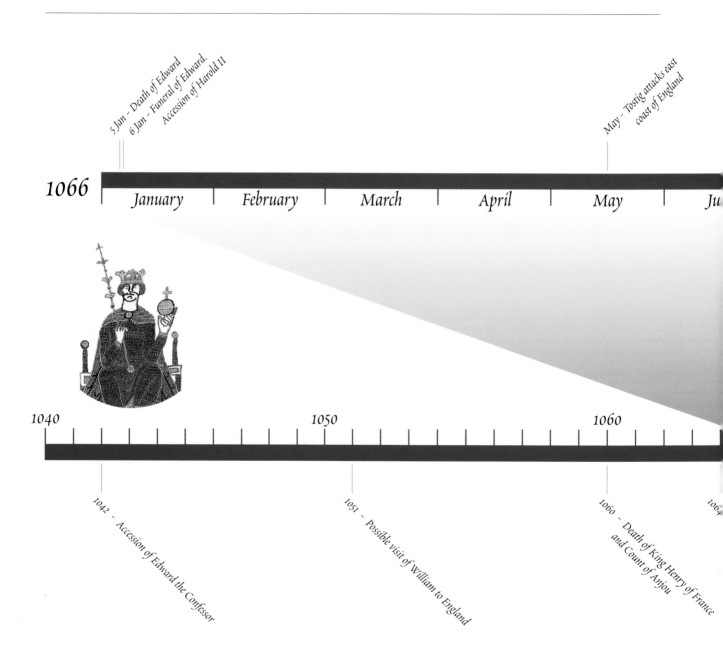

1066

January	February	March	April	May	Ju

5 Jan - Death of Edward
6 Jan - Funeral of Edward.
Accession of Harold II

May - Tostig attacks east
coast of England

1040   **1050**   **1060**

1042 - Accession of Edward the Confessor

1051 - Possible visit of William to England

1060 - Death of King Henry of France
and Count of Anjou

1064

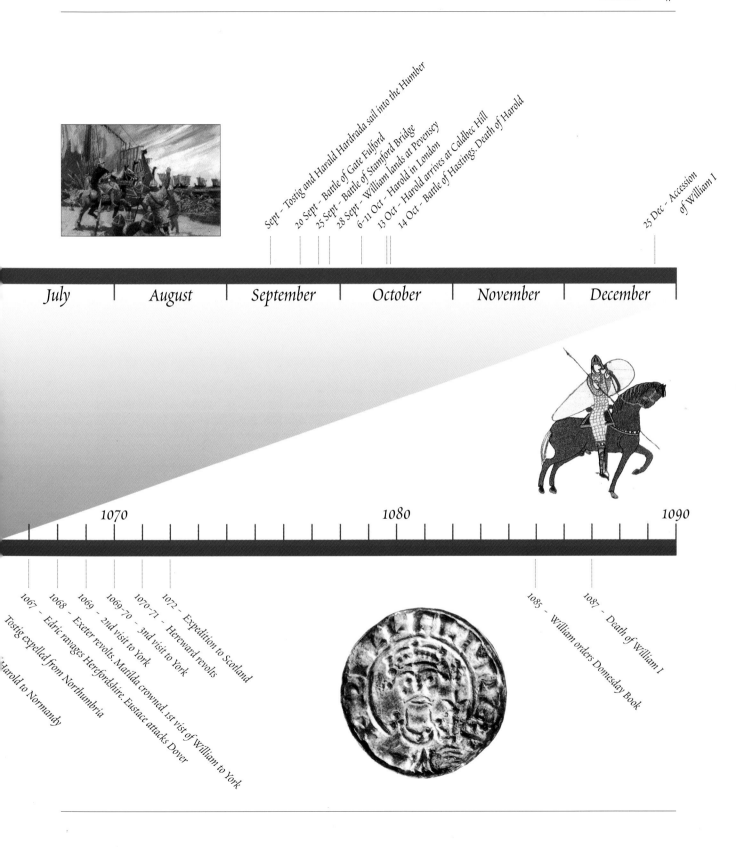

Sept - Tostig and Harald Hardrada sail into the Humber

20 Sept - Battle of Gate Fulford

25 Sept - Battle of Stamford Bridge

28 Sept - William lands at Pevensey

6-11 Oct - Harold in London

13 Oct - Harold arrives at Caldbec Hill

14 Oct - Battle of Hastings. Death of Harold

25 Dec - Accession of William I

July | August | September | October | November | December

1070 | 1080 | 1090

1067 -
Tostig expelled from Northumbria

Harold to Normandy

1068 -
Edric ravages Herefordshire. Eustace attacks Dover

1069 -
Exeter revolts. Matilda crowned. 1st vist of William to York

1069-70 - 2nd visit to York

1070-71 - 3rd visit to York

1072 - Expedition to Scotland

Hereward revolts

1085 - William orders Domesday Book

1087 - Death of William I

First published in Great Britain in 2000 by Osprey Publishing
Elms Court, Chapel Way, Botley, Oxford OX2 9LP

ISBN 1 84176 244 X

Editor: Rebecca Cullen
Designer: Mark Holt

Origination by Valhaven Ltd, Isleworth, UK
Printed through Bookbuilders, Hong Kong

00 01 02 03 04   10 9 8 7 6 5 4 3 2 1

FOR A CATALOGUE OF ALL TITLES PUBLISHED BY
OSPREY MILITARY AND AVIATION PLEASE WRITE TO:

Osprey Direct UK, PO Box 140, Wellingborough,
Northants NN8 4ZA, UK
Email: **info@ospreydirect.co.uk**

Osprey Direct USA, PO Box 130, Sterling Heights,
MI 48311-0310, USA
Email: **info@ospreydirectusa.com**

Or visit the Osprey website at:
www.ospreypublishing.com